Self-Anointment
with Lemons

poems by

Kristiane Weeks-Rogers

Finishing Line Press
Georgetown, Kentucky

Self-Anointment
with Lemons

ACKNOWLEDGMENTS

"Obituary Erasures" first appeared in The Adirondack Review. "Self-Marinate" and "Mexican Drinking Toast" first appear in The Blue Nib. "Spell Against Ghosts" and "Words Are Reassembly" first appear in SurVision. "No Penance" first appeared in Spit Poet Zine.

Thank you family and friends who allow my experiences to take shape, with special thanks to my husband, Richie. Thank you to my Flagler College mentors for holding poetic space in humidity; J.S. and K.B.. Thank you to my IUSB mentor, D.D.L. for bringing out the mysteriousness. Thank you to my JKS poetics guide M.N.P for the push, for believing.

Publisher: Leah Huete de Maines
Editor: Christen Kincaid
Cover Art: Richard Rogers
Author Photo: Richard Rogers
Cover Design: Elizabeth Maines McCleavy

Order online: www.finishinglinepress.com
also available on amazon.com

Author inquiries and mail orders:
Finishing Line Press
P. O. Box 1626
Georgetown, Kentucky 40324
U. S. A.

Table of Contents

To all of us who work as Living Tributes, and to all we've lost.

To Eric and Alex.

And we who loved the world must learn
The language of absence: days foreshortened, empty rooms,
The irrevocable distance
Between the goodbye and the letting go.

Joe Bolton, "Elegy at Summer's End"

Explorations for Closure

Clo·sure
klōZHər
noun   a. a sense of resolution or conclusion at the end of an
artistic work.
b. a feeling that an emotional or traumatic experience has
been resolved.

Defining the word closure
Read an obituary
Don't read an obituary
Read obituary history to rewrite obituaries
Defining words like eulogy, obituary, and elegy
Write obituary-esque poems
Go to a gravesite
Don't go to a gravesite
Make origami
Daily Tarot Draws
Paint flowers
Make paintings out of The Lost's photographs
Paint your favorite tattoo of one of The Lost
Make a shrine
Don't a shrine
Practice meditation
Attempt to find comfort in the gap-zone
Ritualize grief
Don't ritualize grief
Buy a commemorative T-shirt
Don't buy another commemorative T-shirt
Cut up commemorative T-shirt for shrine
Listen to The Lost's favorite songs
Ignore The Lost's favorite songs for two years
Refer to your dead friends as The Lost
Read poetry
Write about anything else
Eulogize
Run away
Circle around for four years

Chain oneself to memory
Attempt to memorialize your friends who didn't live to Thirty
Fail at memorializing your friends who didn't live past Thirty
Redefine "closure"

Salud

Run raw egg
over body,
careful not to crack.

Drop contents
into a glass of filtered water,
watch yolk
observe
opaqueness
through tornado,

it is always in water
there is a call
interpreting you.

Not Enough Ash

When a new frame of language is required
to carry away too-familiar thoughts and feelings,
find scissors instead:

cut out everything that glistens, every glass-given
image which still sticks to your heart. Separate
these blue blips from language which now glows gray.

Put fire to pages on pages of skeletons
out lost at sea, full of sand but not grit—
this is one of the things language can't do,

it can't put sensations into words
when years of life-force arranged from back
to front now furl front to back again.

A moment of silence for cremation
of a language burning, and you let it happen.
It is said the more your paper burns,

the more Spirit is answering prayers.
This must be why beige center of each page
stays full, remains untouched by soft ash.

Guilty Women

There are corn crop circles hiding behind
the backs of everyone in town, bent ovals,

"I don't need all the details," he says.
That's what they always say when a woman

has to explain why she can't bare a child,
tosses a cob in the middle of the symbolic

field. I thought I was ready, able to take
on the slaughtering wolves, rotting seeds…

The stars make me feel guilty, blue with
burning hypotheticals like *if your partner died,*

and you married someone new, would you
possibly want a child then? Would I possibly

want to strangle the light out of my eye sockets
instead? Maybe I could move to Puerto

Escondido and wear all azul…Possibilities,
they're all manipulators. I want tarot cards to

tell me the message in the carefully-laid stalks,
I want the stalks to guide me into lax black

skies, and when I reach to tie a thread around
a white-hot star, there's suffering for it, too.

Procedures, my blood drop. It's so innocent, such
a pie-perfect dab against the sterile floor, how something

that once was, reaching deep into your stomach,
puts a clamp on your cervix. Goya knows

it is eternal: the pressure, the grasp from a heavy

hand that won't let its grip go. It's bottomless,

deep in the center of crop mazes, deep in women
where cold silver wrenches, like a hunched over

boulder beside every abortion clinic, no shelter...
Today, the angry mothers (who didn't have the idea

first) and representatives of wooden crosses aren't
throwing pebbles and condoms at the women

who walk through the doors. The snow is good
for that relief, it keeps all the bears buried below,

although if you crunch gently in the silent woods
after a few inches have fallen and listen

through the glittering wetness, you can tune in to the low
growling. But if you crouch into the tightest ball,

you can fall like the heavy clumps of flakes rolling off
black branches at the lightest breath, separate into moth mist.

To Name

Obituary: a notice of vessel change; Ponce de Leon's espada as judgment of land; stinted red biography.

Eulogy: if I sing a song for you, throw citrus peels around a circle, is this a reverence, flower over dirt, at all?—voices are louder than written words, VOICES ARE LOUDER THAN WRITTEN WORDS, ARE VOICES LOUDER THAN WRITTEN WORDS—

Elegy: dip white rose into tar; attempt to fling out poetry; moan in the night, moan loudly in the night

Flor de Muerte

This skin
vase absorbs stains,
purple light fades as
the living tribute
left behind when love-bodies
are buried into earth. No longer able to see them
as them. I walk the cemetery
to his grave and don't find flowers
picked, but the dandelions will do just fine.

Next day, I walk the cemetery and find
outstretched coral fingers
dropping fruit sack
into my open palms:
three candles, orange, green
black rattle within as it
falls

bouquet stuffed into our mouths.
A snap and then orange,
incredible orange
warm orange of the clay: sun-
rusted
but not flaked, flaking,
just still

over land nature has not yet
let go from.

I try not to listen as it grips me,
orange into stomach
with her dust
saying, "you will rub—
as a dog does
against dead rabbits—
in tall grass,—

hawk picks at prairie dog—
collapse and roll,
you are back and forth—
again and again,
a bouquet you knead
into skin."

No Penance

This, the church
enter through red doors
we are stained crimes, dust
the white pews turn black
and sit.
Enter through red doors
drown in chlorinated holy,
white pews turn black as we sit,
we expect white clean souls.
drown in chlorinated holy,
try to scrub off time,
we expect white like clean souls.
This steeple,
try to scrub off time,
we are stained crimes, dust
this steeple,
this, the church.

Sun-Baked Sky

There's something in
hazy white-blue

heat

it brings out   the sub lime
colors of breathing forms—

forget the usual plethora
green leaves green flowers yellow sun light wind
the summer tags

the blue smears
into
white clarity

lips like skies
disintegrating into   heat

one   two   three...

every seven words   one person dies

looks up at the whiteness
calming blues   discovers black light

oceanic depths   holding her head below

hot summer cars   packing fried babies

and what happens with vibrations after that?

summer's new red sublime shading,
observe how it evokes

one   two   shots from another white man
dicks, guns   (violence and heat don't discriminate

against weapons)

at least schools are out of
session
                    for now

Mexican Drinking Toast

La Catrina's teeth are tucked all over streets
of Mexico; between cobblestones, vendor stands.

Behind smoke-drenched sheets sweeping
a breeze heavy with salt, *toda la sal,*
rimmed glasses we lift up, *arriba!*
her white teeth shine down from shrines,
sculptures, paintings propped on rafters.

Glass down on table, *abajo,* a grounding tap, a hollow call
to her company, hat tipped, dressed even in death;

the streets are blinded by her skirts,
red on blue, on white mixed with subtropic sun,
no wonder she doesn't have eyes,
it's too easy to be blinded, she knows.

Plus her grin angles just right,
reaches out to all, *al centro.*

The bodies in Mexico form a glass circle, clink tequila shots,
drink her smile, hollow bones, eternal hole, al dentro,
assimilate—it is a cycle of toleration, repetition as ritual
get used to the glow, *arriba, abajo, al centro,*

like a dark glow of dusk shining on pane:
al dentro.

Ceremony

The vultures
are dressed in black today

so I shoo them out
back under black pines

black needles stick
into shimmered arms.

Mud like rain over us, in a garden I dig
and dig,

black cicada song as my rhythm,
heart's sound from within

I wedge shiny
corn kernels between wet loam pockets,

lay jade and silver
masks over the mounds.

Low hums reverberate
through me, black bead eyes watching as I re-cover,

give back to deep crevice,
fold feathers tenderly within earth.

To Word the Ways Dusk Stunned Fire

Broken shells make sand beneath us, pull wave hips
whooshing alongside, sticking us together, pushes
from the shore—A distant rumble as clouds
bubble across horizon, muffled sighs against
a pinking sunset over continental edge.

Up in the sky, chariot points to the one fissure
not filling with stars as night consumes.
I see two shooting stars. You see none.
There's nothing empty in all that penetrating velvet
blue-black, when you gaze long enough:
emptiness comforts the stiff breeze.

There's still haze, each other's sweat, humid breaths.
No lightning yet, we watch far-off shrimp boats blink red and cream.
The shore's distant lighthouse looms, stands higher than everyone,
alone on the peninsula, head forever whirs, searches.

During some starfall, we go to a cigar-smoking shack
shrouded in palmetto plants and enough brush
to create coolness in subtropicked weathers
where you recall a dream from last night,
"Estamos dentro con la puerta del balcón abierta,
el sol se está derramando adentro,
Toco la guitarra y te veo en una silla en el sol
como un lagarto en una piedra."

Lemons

I tried to anointment myself with limes once, but the acidity
 astringency wasn't right for skin. So now each morning
I take a sliced-open lemon, close the door and run the shower luke-warm.

I put my hair up, I undress and squeeze gently
toward the segmented-off wound so the juice flows to the rind.
I rub the lemon across the tops of my arms, around my hips
and stand at the end of the shower where the water only rains on my feet.

The more juice, the better.
When you squeeze, it sounds like
Mariachi against cobblestones:
sweet and timber and yellow.

*

The repetition, day to day
same peel, slice, rub
makes re-tracing the groove yours.

Sometimes it stings.
Contact shouldn't last more than five minutes at a time,
but time is imaginary and so are the reasons to keep up some rituals.

I rub a lemon wedge across my brow,
over my cheekbones,
in the folds between nose and face.

Juiced acid slides across pores,
so do tiny pods of citrine pulp.

I love when lemons don't have seeds.

Slow Motion

Ants trail so perfectly behind one another,

hole next to the door lets them wander
to the fridge day after day.

I watch your delicate hands work effortlessly,

grinding white pills with a pink plastic "Rewards
Card" from Dunkin' Donuts.

You drag the card across the table

so meticulously, your rhinestone eyes focused
on the task before you, shaping powder just so…

It's that time, again,

time to wonder if there was ever a day you
weren't sitting at the table snorting

such and such in its linear path to your brain.

Lost in your cosmos, unable to notice all the open spaces.
You explain how this is what you need—

"the planet will be grinding on its axis with or without me"

and then your hair sweeps the table. I watch
the black crumbs file onward

as you bow your head in a moment of silence.

A line of dust soaring, a wave over your eyes. It's that time
of day again, time to forget me, forget

the empires of ants coming to raid, take you.

Hardly Anything Said

Once I asked ghosts
not to haunt me.
I made a deal, I would stop
being a ghost
that haunts others, too.

"Let's let each other be," I said
but they haven't answered, yet.

Their faces do talk flowers
as some distant drip-lined
painting—no, not Monet,
someone wetter.

In the meantime, I let mouths
like carnations fill, watch
sun cross balcony,
Barnett Newman light-lines
cross mahogany floor
left to right,
left to right in slants

while a man outside
hurriedly gusts out
breaths of a cigarette,
then walks
across the railroad tracks.

Watering Lavender

The hen was in the berry basket again
when I came back from watering lavender
watering sage, rosemary; aromatherapy
won't die as long as I'm here to breathe it
but the hen, she twisted unfamiliar
blackberries into her stomach, twisted beak
stained with red. It was my fault
I should have axed the tail over my arm when

I had the chance
now there's no stopping her
no stopping me from ravishing
fat succulent blackberries
the berry basket has never been full,
it never will be, except full of the hen

What can't I do with an egg? Put the shell
back together yolk, membrane, all
pick up the broken fragments of shell
what if I used sugar-glue? At least
something sweet and delicate like the hen's shell

I don't think there's a remedy for that.

Origin of My *Envidia*

Limber limbs
reach for Himalayan
pink salt blocks
stuck in the mouth

Cynical Saint
with all the loam collected
cultivating forms of
browned lace
trampled with boot prints

delicate designers
we take your contentious
credence, oaths to
anchor us to the loam

slouching towards Babylon
to be offered grace

Oh, we make
much of our own suffering,
it's our fault, it's my fault

we make mountains of
our suffering, the weight
of the anchor, of the spirit

Forget your blessings
they've forgotten you

Don't give me
the choice, Baby
I will always choose

the fall

A Way To Spot *Envidia*

In the evening you unlock
new apartment with fresh set of keys.

There is no furniture, yet,
so you sit in the windowsill

watch bar-bodies sway back and forth
across the street like toddlers

a light sprint
a car

a body like rumpled paper—
not red.

As you turn from the scene,
drop below frame—
Still hear screech of car
still feel body
as a bag
cars still pass
sirens finally groan.

As you turn from the scene,
blue and red
flashes through giant Victorian windows,
doesn't fill the gap—
permeation of space
as dimensions crack open.

As you turn from the scene,
feel suspension of time
for days
after the violet layer takes a body
into its elsewhere.

Healing Will Not Look the Way You Want It To

I was seven when death's deflation scarred my eye sockets.
It wasn't opposite, only altered like every Mariachi band

dressed in golden velvets, ringing brass hearts so loud
the dead in us all quake. Energy passes between the sweet song

celebrating breath in every petal, alchemy of color, now absence—
My father holds me by the bones, leads me under limelight

to a dead shiny fir fashioned for shiny purple lips, pearls,
no white wings. *The darkness is just a different form of light...*

I'm such an admirer of the soft glow of skulls now
I cradle one in my head at all times. Sometimes it will

remind me it's closed away, yet close by; it knocks
against my teeth, swirls knots through my hair. Sometimes

it will ask me to give it a silk ribbon to play with, instead
I give it matchboxes, ask it to make firecrackers for lips.

Cenote

I've read more suicide attempts, wishes, plans
on paper than the hospital has:
I don't write this seeking sympathy or
not desiring anything or
without dance, what is there?
this is what it looks like,
how it feels when a cave collapses:

Soft like whitened limestone,
water is heavier than sky
no matter where you are:
Lake Michigan, Clear Creek, Matanzas Bay,
Bahia de Banderas. How many
have gone heavy-blue breathless?

Bluing sacredness unknown, breath is
easier when held. Wait for land
to drop out from beneath—whose feet
are we praying will buckle open
first? Salt lips create
a gape: violet silences
these feet fall into (willingly).

My feet search for soft spots
on cool damp ground,
watch city lights on rolled hills
twinkle in the dark from a distance
for hours, a violet silence rings—
soft like limestone, bodies are natural pits.

Map of Curses

Envidia in Mexican folk medicine interprets
to bad luck placed on you by someone else, a curse
intentionally set by someone else—

Not exactly a painting of a boy which won't catch fire;
or a doll which seems to laugh
with no touch
but to be touched—orange horizon line
cut through green without prompt,
salted hands stretch through
my open sight—

Only twenty-five percent of Americans
think their houses are haunted,
but I'm willing to bet there's
millions more. The types of haunting are infinite,
these old or new houses
black creak or beige tapped,
whispers from a wall, or houses built
on or over sacred lands, cursed lands.

The haunted houses with figures darker
than the dark or sitting on chests in dreams,
the houses which are haunted houses
the houses that are haunted persons
the houses which have one (or many) haunted
dolls, masks, skulls, boxes, baubles.
The haunted houses who have changed the floor
plan, locked the extra room, plowed through basements.
The houses built with recovered stone
from prison, the house which used to be a sanitarium.
The houses sitting on coasts where every boat crashed,
the houses which used to be butcheries,
the houses where we are the butchers,
the houses where we are the butchered,

memories and glasses and photographs,
we are all haunted by something.

Omens

Watermelon cubes
filled up the plastic cup

that was advertised as "sangria"—
watermelon cubes with dots of blueberries
and citrus pulp

Most of the cubes you spit at
crows and passing cars,

the pattern of the seeds warns us,
oncoming rain showers

gray and blue drops catch on
his curled eyelashes, they look so long

we make a break for it, find shelter
under an abandoned ticket station

the tin roof applauds our escape
from the summer shower

we wait for the drops to pass and
watch as a crow pecks at a sparrow

until the sparrow and the shower both
stop rattling. The crow carries

the limp sparrow into high branches
of a nearby tree, then flies away.

Sentinel

The nightmares show
two boys standing in the salty Matanzas

One has his father's golden
Almond—shaped eyes
the other
Still holds shades of new—born
baby blue

One is blowing bubbles through
a nine-o-tails made of chain links
his golden eyes furl at the corners,
wrinkle into snaring, snarls

the other boy chases
swings a sickle
back and forth
back and forth

but then a warm breeze passes
carrying soapy orbs high
out of harm's way,

a wind that whispers
extinguish all endangerment
before it's too late.

Spell to Ward off Negativity

There is no white spell
to recover language.
I've researched every
website
book

Curendera in Mexico City
could only offer me *Toloache,*
no green tincture
or herbs to summon
primordial chromosome
deep within this body

wash like red apples in jasmine oil,
set tongue aside at entrance
of home;

wring from this hair
concoction
of *origen—*
prefix to suf-
fix,

buds like apples
absorb
as much negative energy
as they can, bruise
along the way.

Poetics of the Gap

Guilt spills out when a part
of you dies and you're not there
to let it go, ocean-heavy
like a chrysanthemum
contrived from salt-licks,
cut loose from some strand
never there to begin with, mouthed opaque chrysalis.
Hands aren't hidden
around the square,
they are visible
limestoned
on platforms and reach out
of steeple tops
where we can't reach,
but keep reaching toward
as we grasp around each other.

I ran when the crime came hot on the cheeks,
but what good is nostalgia now
(or ever)?
The greatest nostalgia is writing poetry after
reading someone else's poem.
Trying not to copy every
lost beauty restored—
Who cares if it's already been said
it needs to be said, again,
again with different
breath and integrity:
and water
is as empty
as sky,

and water is as empty as sky!

and water is
as empty as
sky.

Write to Cope

fuck every
time I kept
myself
from

unraveling

there, I finally
wrote into solid
matter

nothing
is like

unraveling

skin, intestines, blue veins
turn to

octopi, roots

faces

all of my worried

faces

transform

eyes koi hummingbirds

and hands

only shells bones
coagulate
keep me
in now

Obsequies

Not some coin-purse
sack of burlap
stuffed with T-shirt
fragments or gold-frame
Aviator/sunglass lens,
not a blip note
in a newspaper left to yellow—

Our dead turn ghost
to haunt through us,
to turn toward open mouths
open gestures
living tributes

our ghosts become words.

Yet words are bound orbs
in a soft, damp space
with peach-scented candles,
messages are unwound clocks
underwater
with purple starfish.

Letters buried
beneath wrinkled brown
hands, are decaying
next to wet earth
and turquoise eyes
closed when you left,
unwound,

left to uncover,
uproot black orchids
to discover new meaning
of life without you,

words are reassembly of bone.

Sombras Borrachas

I know what
makes a person
turn into heavy shadow,
dissipate at dawn,
no return—but if
they do,
they come back
at different angles.

Ice on spine then
from elbow to biceps
is how the dead begin
to live again.

This time
in you

…Grief appears different each time
full-red wasted,
this is prototypical slur
against clinked-up glassware.
A yellowed glow from within,
a yellowed hand tap

another day gone
to cracked music,
a needle grind—
ground through…

This is hardly
making a sound

frail soot, now.
How gentle we must be
when someone else depends
in us.

Lengua

If words are reassembly
of skeleton,
which white bones
do I pull *lengua* from?
I ask my father
my *abuela*
my self

no one can remember where—

Reclaim
plummeted branches
from oldest *Ahuehuete* at dusk
as red fingers blot out
a tongue
generations forgotten—

I, thin green strip off-
center
fallen but
lifts then,
to seep into the red
just barely,
barely.

Tarot Reading

What to expect from me: you
know when you'll know.

The only thing I have ever done
was to make a huge batch of coffee
with a few pages in my area.
Poets, blind eyes painted
silver for centuries,
ancient method to cleanse—

quartz ground into antidotes
for hardened hearts out of luck.
We caved at the same night
like this new world

to reach/eat in a place, dream of being able
to talk about blue, we can
switch your fingers to loam-stained
at this dinner table then…

begin with an aesthetic look

but it will not help. Don't bring bodies,
only ash to pass
to others, smear around

brow and mouth without incantation,
silent homage
to broken features formed… Sun erupts without our help,
so you still light the incense
and I still hide the dagger.

The only way you can find a card that isn't terrible
for the week, the company

is through some different types of heart
full of wanted lake city

young and then there.

It's here. The carrying act
is really a little crazy,
but it looks good on you.

Spell Against Ghosts

My father once told me,
"Corn is a spell for the dead,"
letting the magic
slip into object

which surrounds
my Indiana-grown youth.
I begin to hide red kernels
in my pockets,

finger them when
I feel scared,
I just chant over and
over,
corn to bring you after life,
corn for continued life,
corn for continued life,
corn to bring you after life

Obituary Erasures

Eric   of Gaine   , Flor da, pass   22, 2015.
      born   Ea t   ogue,   came here
              I land,   He   Faith.   rently
                                                    Planet   s
      coach for   body.   beginning   ache
pro   become   acher,   who   teach   us all
      From   day   he aught   meaning   love,
                  dy   e import   of f   ily,   blings   out
            ship. He l   spo ts, especially   ll.
love   fight   s   a d   others   self   t e th
er d   . One   favori   o   w   ive as   k   e   d   tomorrow.
earn   you   to   o ver."
        survive   by   other, Mi   risti   of Crystal River:
      orey   rist   sters,   dice   and aige   sins,
            on,   fr   e   sh   w   i   tt   a d,
      fro   s   w   i   th   out

/
Alex   Cha   pass   unexpect   July 24, 2016.   leaves
be   his lov   e   my Craft   grand
Joy   Do   a nts   za ne   (aura Baker),
Wells,   raft   lop   and Lin
                    sins   fer Wells,   itch
        chu   s   or   ceased
Me   Fall   ather   sin
              ex   25   ille,   or   up in
      August   here   n e   e   d
              rad. be   U   t   Flor
                          b   o   y w   u   n
        t   w   a   w A   I t   Systems
for   just   nior   mation Engin   arm s
Insur   e   les,
           irky   mor   e   new   hilario
            oof   capacity   ness   ship crossed
      walks   busi   w   i t U   s
        t   ar   s   happ e   n frequent   n
                    o   la st   no ledge

36

write for   so a p   in edibly   lent
            young   lead   in the world   m
      mmunity.
//

here   **I land,**
Er   o   , passe   2015.
        or   Ea t   gue,   here
            I land,   H   currently
        ent   Plane
        ach
                            come   ache   who   ach   s
            From   he   meaning
                    dy   e i port   of f   i   bling   out
        ship. He l   special
love   fight   others   self   t e th
    er d   favor   ive as   k   e   d   morrow.
                you   o ver."
        survive   by   Mi   Crystal   ive
    rey   st   dice   and   sins,
            on   fr   e   sh   w   i   tt   a d
    frot   s   wi   i   th   out
the country
/

be Un   t Fl   b   o y w   u   n   t w A   I t

A   a   a   expect   2016   leaves
                lov   e   my
Joy   s   a ne
Wells,   raft   in
                    sins   itch
        chu   se
                Fall   in
                ex   ill   up
    August   here   n e   e   d
                rad. be   U   t   Flo
                            b   o y w   u;   n
        t   w   a   w A   I t   Systems

for   just   nior   mation Engine   arm   s
Insur   e   les,
          irky   mor   e   new   hilario
            oof   capacity   ness   ship crossed
      walk   busi   w   i t U   s
      tt   ar   s   happ e   n frequent   n
                        o   la st   no ledge
write for   so a p   in edibly   lent
            young   lead   in the world   m
community.

//

fr   e   sh   to death
E   pass   2015.
                                                              here
            land,   H   Fait   ent
                                                  Plan
          for   ache
                                                  who   us
                                                        meaning
                                          of f
      ship.
love   others   t e th
  er d   ive as   kou   e   d
            you   o ver."
                                                        Crystal
      rey   st   sins,
                  fr   e   sh   with   out
            t   o   w   i   th   out

/

w   u   n   t w A   I t

A   2016.   leaves
                        my
                  s   a ne
Wells,

ill

be U t Flo
b o y w u n
t w a w A I t
for u
les
mor e
capacity ship crossed
w i t s
t ar s
no ledge
write in edibly
young lead in the world

Sílaba

Syllables linger like sand—appear in floor-cracks
by washing machine,
stick in trunk-fabric of car,
mue-, crá-, escar-

I can't reach deeply enough into these porous fields
to retrieve, examine collage
of peach speckles, black shark's tooth,
foreign fragments.

Syllables linger like Spanish moss
on tallest limbs of Family Tree.

How Far Back Can You Remember?

In the spirit house, I am alone.
Inescapable, the way out found by looking in
down through the rafters—only shrieking,

no shimmer, sorry, Ashbery. Sorry
Asheville, I can't stay. Your hidden black
bears, disheveled Black Mountain

are too obvious reminders of all we've lost.
Next day I find a single scarlet Carolina leaf
and when I pick it up, it pulls me

from the fabric world. The lesson: *all memories
are generic spectres of truth.* Maybe that's
why I miss you. There are so many
secrets in the spine of Appalachia,

I've been trying to tap them out, over-turning
musk-covered peaks to catch a clue, finding
a longing with nothing left to long for

except ennui and burned up roaches. Mixed
tea leaves and heart beat so loud: muddle
into a sedative as soft counterweight. Then I hear

your footprints call my name, but your eyes will
turn to orchids waiting for my signal back—everything
is an imaginary reason to keep holding out for more.

Shaken and Stirred

Frank O'Hara said after the first glass of vodka, you can accept
just about anything of life, even your own mysteriousness, but what if

your body can't accept the Vodka? My grandparents didn't sail
from Prussia for me to form a worming stomach, but I didn't design

my innards: slow-roasted swine on the birch pole, glazed skin falling off
as it tenderizes, with time as the perfect marinade. Mysteriousness believes

my intestines glow, twinkling Christmas lights on twine, twinkling
from all the black holes along the way, twigs falling from careful beaks

of birds building a nest nestled between branches of my ribcage,
relentless motion. My own mysteriousness can be summed up: blue grass

in Indiana, crab grass at the feet—the classic one-two jab to the jaws
of every goose-necked bottle that's passed through ancestral hands…

At least I can lie in the soft blues of you, Indiana, since my feet carry
no balance and, sure as hell, we know Vodka never let anyone stand

on theirs without willowing in the wind like long confetti-colored streamers…
vodka-bodies, the only ones who aren't reaching for spindled clouds,

rolling like gemstones in brown streams. When we were climbing up
Chimney rock, I refused to drink until we reached the peak, then I drank

it all in. The river, such a sparkling small intestine hiding under
cancers of green puffs, exposed aging sediments and calcium snuck

between cracks in the mountain's heart. We cannot love the stone forever;
the trees won't allow such exposure, no excavating their bones, or ours.

Can't Mix the Sun with the Earth

Mashing boiled apples with peaches, he says
there's no better way to mix the sun
with the earth. This baked dough boy, sugar
falls in lumps from his body to the floor

as he shuffles around, gathering spices,
mixing basins, ingredients of comfort.
He sings *an apple pie without cheese*
is like a kiss without a squeeze—suddenly

I know he's right, and every other hot oven
has been baking all wrong, all these years.
The same way painters can't mix acrylics
with tin foil to get the orange, the taupe

shaded right, the same way relocating
to Florida has never really cured anyone
of melancholia or hysteria, *Barry's Florida Water*
bottles broken all along the coquina streets...

The advertisements said this state cures land-
locked syndrome, but there's actually nothing
worse for you: standing on a clinging shore,
afraid to get your blouse wet, afraid

of the heaviness of cloth, the truth of wet salt—
there *is* nowhere else to go without a paddle.
There's one path of sunken footprints you
came from, soft cupped hands, not feet.

So you follow them in reverse, although nothing
else is also in reverse, unfortunate paths. This
must have been what drove Joe Bolton: sinking
crusted fingers, smell of salt stuck to every

thing. His dried-out veins and constant sting
of open wounds. Sulfur water can only cleanse

black water back to black. It can cure longing
for nutmeg or any wish to escape sink holes,

a common feature of the landscape with lost villas,
cars, and bodies included. There's one humid
balloon in the sky, it hovers the haunted Atlantic
breezes, won't carry me, won't carry Joe away.

Stone Breaking

There is no blue world, only the time line and the place where you realize the
    stones
mark your spot, tossed in when you aren't paying attention
stones kicked, axed, thrown, it doesn't matter, the stones
there can't help you,
when you fall from
atmospheres you won't be created, pressed into
comets or sea glass,
there is nothing.
I wanted rescue and I wanted again and

ghosts know that the stones will break
them, a trillion new tinging
pink particles for the stars,
upside down cycle made just for those ethereal
skins
hanging, fresh meat
above the clouds, salivation,
ethereal mouths of multiple colors—does it matter? It's the only
thing that really worries them: destined to shape the helplessness of us.

Vultures

There is ecstasy of sunshine tracing equator
it enters into skin
like cocaine enters bloodline, not ready to discharge.
Arms, long wings we use to float
on thermal hazed glow
as I cross cobblestone streets
ripe with scent of citrus, cinnamon-chocolate.

We gorge ourselves on Southern
delicacies, stuffed piñatas
until moon joins us. During dark
we find a different warmth
listening for lost children:

signal to us with singing from a higher tower,
eye whirring around, searches for other specters
in dustspray, wind keeps flowing.
Too terrified to let this beacon go,
circle like vultures
without a syrinx to say otherwise…

And sure as sunrise,
we continue, all dress our bodies
and emerge again into hot haze of sun over
pulped limes in gutter.
Chipped buildings somehow still allure,
pastel cream mints
waiting to be eaten from glass bowl,

how am I supposed to leave these badlands
since witnessing her bare & raw, enchanting charm?

Tongue-Tied

A flower, just before the bloom,
the way all the buffered blossoms
aren't building to make a scene

like lips or fingers not ready to take the plunge,
can't get themselves to unfurl until

morning light, or perhaps until the
wind has waxed between the bed
frame and the watering pot, words are

petals origami-tight. Canoes not
willing to take any weight on board,
except a few brave vessels, open,

slow lambs ears pushing from a
thousand fuchsia mole noses all
pointing toward photosynthesis, all

contemplating, shaking at the bud.
There will be no sprouting today,

no laying out the vases full of tap.
Water has to hide in the pumps for
now, until I can wrench the bulbs

open, clear my throat for pollen.
Until I forget the right words will
refuse to take root in still water.

Salt Cathedral

Upside down roses painted peach,
braids curving some setting sun

in eyelids. Everyone holds
the downward gaze, constant

sun ringing in the visor... or
something more interesting

in the ground below, but that's
obvious. All the colors, stems

popping up from dirt-soaked
secrets mixing with veins, it's more

than she can bare, lights up just
one more Nat Sherman—

smoke dancing diamonds
around salt-carved saints.

Funnel Ghost

Soulless—something beyond what
ever it is you perceive. String it out,
unwinding tunes that shape momentary
movement between earth, falling stars

falling into a lull. Even with a mouth
full of words, my heart's too weak
to keep suppression hidden, but too
young to burst. It's difficult for you

to keep away, get stuck out or…
are you in? Heartsick fingers can't claw
through the grave's rich loam,
glowing softer, more comforting

the longer we wait for the moon
to reel us in. Instead, I'll play
with red tide, wait for summer
to sink so I can sink too…

Everything is a ritual, sacrament of time:
Listless ramblings under a blood sun

too close to the horizon-line.

Your eyes were made to fool you—

refractions, upside-down lies make the sun appear
large and close enough to swallow the world,

O, if it just would, already

so all the flowers can stop fearing

if it's going to happen, just accept the warmth pressed
against core.

The Cursed

Through setting suns or surrounding
yourself with copper for spiritual
conductivity, there's no clear

difference. It's seven a.m., my head's
filling too loudly, heart's still beating
the same. When it's not skipping,

it's sunken, deflated vessel fashioned
from ribs. The sentiment doesn't age,
but the intention does, still, there's

starlight reflecting in the lake. Phantom
heartache leaps, and leaps again, listen
to taps on the rooftops—then the wind picks

up. *We are remains of something long
torn-apart.* Dissection left to rest, to find
mortar from energy exchanging between
us. Friction-driven, only glimmer left

that doesn't need to be tested for acidity:
too much weight on my ribs—keep pulling
at the sutures… There's no fable telling

why it happens: every night after five stars
prick early evening skies, a ghost
who can't remember its name appears

playing an ivory violin. If you don't
bring it to bed with you, its skeleton
won't let you sleep ten days straight.

Quicksilver Solution

As artificial as suns,
they won't take away
hands clambering

against chills brought
by reinforcement
day-cycles without rules—one, two,

another poet goes down.
Not here for her...
So we are tides

against Fire Island,
restless and changing easily,
born in pain—

I feel it everywhere, now,
missing a good scene of red,
don't squirm—

Stir to get skin over rapids
slicing through a face
in the cracks of mountain-

sides, breaking glass
using tools to understand
methodology, no biological possibility,
I can't feel anything, it's fine...
Terrible things come in threes,
this time through

a constant tinge of trying
to bring his blue
eyes out of the green river.

Cimientos

In primary school I practice spelling words with my mother,
she tells me I use my tongue too much.

In graduate school I practice Spanish in front of a friend,
their instruction repeats:
use your tongue more.

Architecture of Cemetery Earth

Adorn your eyelashes, paint
and napalm. Your ankles
lace up with scarlet ribbons:
ghost trail behind soft steps.

Carry this bayonet,
sewing needle through
your dress. You, shrouded

in new blue light on stage.
You can only see blue
light and the moon as it breaks,
tossed with dust and rocks,

it's thick blood falling away
from us, down… Another shroud.
It probably didn't take long
for the dead to outnumber the living
but we keep pretending it's not true—
Now what do we do? Now what

can we do? We all prick lunar
pieces from the ruins, carefully
select what crumbs we'll still
choose to believe in.

The Seer

Fraudulent sights, like
a palm, you unravel

pulling everything apart.
Done with fluttering

"All in your mind…"
It's so much more

terrifying to display
empty sockets than

an empty heart—darkness
staring, or never fully

developed in the first
place. Oh, I'll take the risk,

won't take the fall for it.
Silver stripes don't

understand it's not only
about the road, but

the war… Just haunt me,
don't hold me, after all.

Family Tree Shakes

We keep going back to the cemetery, turn graves
upside-down, we can see feet
of the underworld this way,
we can still grasp pink toes, wash feet
and roots we lost along the way,
pray they won't

disintegrate into earth for good. What, besides bones,
can we keep as tribute?

Burn copal over coal in ceramic *incensario*, smoke skin in badlands
perform *limpia*, cleanse,
through sweet basil, pepper trees—

Creaking whispers,
though we aren't listening, thump-thumping,

though we aren't breathing the way our father told us to:
"Your magic is the energy, stems from behind"—
slough sanctified sands from spirit
with sliced limes,
his timbre voice lines the crown-

molding of the house, but the foundation has
disappeared... I burn copal over coal
in ceramic *incensario*, white water

perform this *limpia*, wave herbs in air
toward North, for Earth
patroned-voice calls from southern wind,

but can't strip grit from *alma,*
manos atadas
en origen.

You Should Stay Away From Here, There are Ghosts

Stone says *you ate the soul,*
now you have a body— but
it doesn't really work that way:

ignore touch, mindless
rotations of fingers to skin,
ginger mixed with tequila.

The trick is you have to want
it more than you fear it,
follow the silver thread to

the epicenter. Just don't look
back because you're not
going that direction anymore…

Self-Marinate

On the way to Anejo,
I am in a thick glass bottle plopped in Kentucky Blue grass,
hand-blown and a little-off with bubbles obstructing
some view of woman waiting for the right time
to get past mother…

On the way to extra anejo
I must travel through opacity, through ghosts across walls or sun drenched
    deserts,
Written ghosts processed as pages and pages and pages
over gold, there must be flexibility
to wander these tunnels,
sharpness or willingness to stay a while,
find some space like encased self in trunk of oak,
marinating is an aspect
of self I rely on, the better with age
(and maybe yearning impatience).

Take a gulp, it takes time to discern salt from spice
swish in circles, swish in circles, despite my disdain for getting ocean in my
    mouth.

I like when things shine as you turn them, shake them up to get at all angles,
when you swirl a bottle of tequila, the liquid moves in lines
as copper wires transmitting knowledge
through metallics, through light, through viscosity…

Take a gulp to feel fire blankets from within,
clinkle of teeth, a caramel voice is the spark
worth waiting to reveal.

Reclamation

The largest tattoo on my body
is a classic portrait of Our Lady of Guadalupe,
patron saint of Mexico
with two distinct differences.

One: instead of an angel at her feet, there is a sacred heart
containing the initials of my parents: G & T.

Two: the banner "Our Lady of Guadalupe" under the portrait isn't in English
nor is it Spanish. This banner reads: *Matki Bozej z Guadalupe*—Polish.

The permeation of my mother, of her power to convert my father to Catholicism,
to convert our Mexican nuances, alter frame—
Virgen de Guadalupe
Reina de Mexico
Salva nuestra Patria
Conserva nuestra Fe!—
She is under the feet of Guadalupe.

Reclamation of self is to rebuild
what others have stripped away,
I am the sparkle-filled sequence of something
long torn apart, dissection
left to rest, not to reconcile
what is lost with what is left,
craters shine
where culture should be—

How can I possess your lost skin, *abuela,*
ink language
on outermost cavities,
Calavera
and Our Lady of Guadalupe
firmly to each
thigh.

downslope windstorm

you sleep where gusted winds
are likely,
outside
five seconds

of finding the right
slit not allowing darkness
to take the room.
night is not
lonely

with mountains
to the west,
ghosts all
to the east, far

behind—
what else is keeping you awake?
count carcasses

across beige range
swirled
with transparent rivers,
meteorite paths…

with a roared
arrival,
overnight guests

come as creaks and
metallic tings,
a train
like canned music
through wooden chairs

up on tables echoing

your dream
running through
lit cigarettes
looking out the window

at the rockies...
squall lasts

until dawn
by the time
you recognized your own
bag of bones,

say to own shadow,
"you look good in black."

You Are a Perishable Item

Throw us a bone or five. We can use the marrow, build
new cathedrals from the remains, use sparklers for our

preachers. They flash, gold streaks in a smooth corner,
forgetting there's no glorious suffering in amber glitter.

Knock-out stars all rising, disappear into earth. It's as good
as any hiding place, but not for protection… There is comfort

in glass mandala windows, facets, all embers and scarlets,
etched blue palms shining in the center. They show us more

than black spaces between heart beats can, build up more
than we lose. Create, then watch our bodies, our own palms

turn blue. Then Supreme Buddha enrobed in fountains
tells us, *No need for this wax disco, even fish eventually*

drown (licks the icing from the mourning cake). Now
that we're never going back, there's no use for eyes.

Incantation

Cardinal feather & sage bundle smoking in the sill, ritual to find any answer:
I feel the same, not changing as fast as Midwestern skies: white, bleak, then
gray haze & they wonder why so many teens are choosing to medicate & blink
out instead of droning through the crossroads of Nowhere - Dirt Road, but
is it really so difficult to empathize? & how many more are done with waking
to aching sunshine, feeling half of who you are or can be, unable to wash out
demands from our throats, shape incantation into action..?

I see them, trying to find the soft grip of moon waning, wanting to spool threads
of stars around it, their bluing fingers, their disarticulated bones without air to
spiral through lungs, expel. From the fire, can't make clay; from heartstrings,
we find only witnesses with the rough touch of something faint that won't stay
in the catastrophe of the past. *& they say if someone leaves it's best to know
why, & I know why you both left, so what am I supposed to do with all the left-
over drugs? How am I supposed to leave Death since witnessing her bare & raw,
enchanting charm?*

Aimless. Down to shores of Ana Island like some wishful fools off to find the
Fountain of Youth (11 Magnolia Ave.), feel flood tides crash against crumbling
seawalls again and again, crash and crash again. Not getting any better at
resistance…

> a weekday outside the Magic Beach Motel: stars keep shooting off behind
> Eric's head; pink yellow white, pink yellow tings with tequila
> chain-smoke while he tells us about future plans (memorials now)

> > another sunset down the gutter, how every Floridian's
> > night begins, antique muffled voices all born unlucky
> > with skin (rub salt over the shoulders, repeat daily…)
> > I imagine littering my feathers behind, the world taking

> > > a long drag
> > sigh heaving, ocean crash somewhere nearby

A long drag, crash and crash again as I bring shears, tear into memories of
chipping seafoam faces: all the days thinking of those bluing eyes, thinking
of those waves cross-country, thinking of giving you guys up or joining you,
no longer caring about direction or light. In dreamscapes, translucent hands
try breaking every expectation the sun will rise again tomorrow, O, so tired of

circling the same track of cosmos, every day…

        another Thursday, after the psychic reader on Bernard Street

        performs her fifth reading flipping Ace of Pentacles

then she walks into the Atlantic, pod of sea weed washing up in her place

            more memorials. Mouths stay close but closed off

          like stretched badlands along arid shores,

                   eyes doing more swimming,

                   learning to see with salt clumped to eyelashes.

—Should I have gone long ago?

            Cardinal feather and sage bundle smoking in

the sill.

La Polilla

Those falling, like a leaf
flittering down
to the ground you notice
out of the corner of your eye.

When you look down
you see a weightless white moth,
wings stretched out in perfect
symmetry with gray designs
matching its concrete grave.

You want to pick it up
but you just look at it,
knowing it's too late.
It's dead and there's nothing
that can change this fact.

Distance is a tool
used to isolate
and it feels like miles between
your eyes and the moth.
The miles take you farther
and farther apart.

This time, let it stretch you out.

Giving up the [   ]

Gestures open to turn toward open mouths, our dead turn
  to haunt through us, living tributes as our [ ] become words, as
  skeletons are the "strewn throughout pseudo-physical being"
  like how I've written the word so much that I can't write it anymore,
  looks wrong letters not belonging next to one another, this sequence—

Haul: burn old words which don't create— I made a deal, I would stop where
your   teeth come out like stars, a manic [ ] along hazy shore
  haunt of others, too…

you should stay away from here, there are [ ]
  white-hot, rising out
  all
  to the east, a funnel who doesn't know its name begins to dry
  and come out, grasp onto sunbeams in your palms.

Once I asked all the shimmering not to haunt me. They rise from cool of the
  mountains, striped
  limestone and calcium from ground antlers and Cherokees. I must travel
  through that opacity: through, across
  walls or sun-drenched deserts,
  [ ] written as pages and pages and pages
  Processed, I need a
Spell against what words bloom from decayed ground besides black/curse,
badland, gap, hole,
  contra, suffocate…

To write is to be skin still stuck in limbo, lace up with scarlet ribbons, mouths
  trail behind soft steps. Take a tour through remaining wooden
buildings   in too-narrows streets:
Shimmering, still. Every shimmering thump is why bridges are supposed
  to burn: some never die.

Kristiane Weeks-Rogers (she/her/hers) is a Poet-Writer among other titles such as copy editor and book reviewer. She is the 2nd place winner of Casa Cultural de las Americas and University of Houston's inaugural Poetic Bridges contest, which also produced the limited chap collection Become Skeletons published by the University of Houston in 2018.

She was born in South Bend, Indiana and grew up around Lake Michigan. Throughout childhood, she always loved reading modernist and postmodernist authors, favoring the poets of the New York School and Beat movements. She traveled South and earned her Bachelor's degree in English literature with a minor in Creative Writing at Flagler College. She then spent some time back in the Midwest to earn her Master of Arts in English Composition at Indiana University.

Always striving to climb up the ladder, when she officially moved west of the Mississippi, she earned her MFA at Naropa University's Jack Kerouac School of Disembodied Poetics in Boulder, Colorado. As a part of the Naropa University family, Kristiane performed an original song titled "Ginsberg" on Allen Ginsberg's birthday in this lineage's honor in 2017 at Boulder's Fox Theatre.

Colorado is where she continues to live now as a Senior Poetry Editor for the online publication *Harbor Review*. She enjoys hiking, creating art, giving a platform to those who are not privileged to have one, and drinking coffee and libations around the Rocky Mountains with her husband and dog while discovering what ghosts really are.

Website: kristianewrites.wordpress.com
Email: kk.weeks.rogers@gmail.com
Instagram: @kosmicallykonnected

www.ingramcontent.com/pod-product-compliance
Lightning Source LLC
Chambersburg PA
CBHW021158090426
42740CB00008B/1147